Also by Fawna Bews:
Finding Fawna: Using Cancer for Awakening

The Circle of Trust
Shift to Healthy Relationships

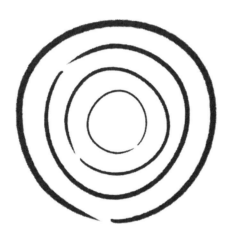

Fawna Bews

ISBN 978-1533168177
© 2016 by Fawna Bews Edition 1
Illustrations by Paige Bews
Edited by Gail Edey
Technical Advice and Paige motivation by Jake Bews

For My Children,
Jake, Paige and Gus, brilliant souls.

Introduction

Opening a book about healthy relationships implies a few things. You believe that there is such a thing. You believe that there may be a way to get there and you are willing to give it a try. This alone holds great power, the most important part of change has already happened! You can now rest easy and enjoy the book.

I hope to illuminate the perceptions that interfere with healthy relationships. Healthy relationships are our natural state and anything that interferes is a misperception that can be corrected. When we know where we are coming from then, like any journey, we can plan where we are going and how we are going to get there.

I am intending to write from a place of Truth. A place where blame and shame have no home. Join me in setting blame and shame to the side while you read. Explore different points of view and finally make an informed choice on how you want to see the world. The choice is in your hands. The choice to have healthy relationships lives inside of you.

The information in this book has developed gradually. I was born into a family that has always done 'care work'; in 1975 my Grandpa, Mervyn Edey, started a 'Ranch for Boys' with the belief that anyone can have a successful life if they are given a chance. He believed that he knew what kids needed; to have freedom, to be fed well and to be surrounded by supportive and caring adults. This program ran for 38 years and over 1500 kids. After the three original boys had difficulty assimilating in the local public school, my Dad, at my Grandpa's request, started a school at the Ranch. When Grandpa Merv grew too ill to run the program my parents assumed management. Management came to a third generation in 2012, it was passed on to me and my brothers and we made the difficult decision to close our doors in 2013. The work that we did at The Stampede Ranch for Kids was influential in my current world view.

I started my own career as a Physical Therapist but when my clients started to share their personal and emotional issues with me I was not prepared. I made the decision to take my Masters in Counseling while starting my family in the hopes that I could contribute to the Ranch program and to understand my physiotherapy clients more fully. My work was interrupted in January 2000, my Master's degree still fresh, with an 18 month old girl and a 2 ½ year old boy. I was diagnosed with Stage IV Non-Hodgkin's Lymphoma. Emergency treatment for this was a clinical trial of High Dose Chemotherapy, a Stem Cell Transplant and radiation (with Chinese Medicine, Acupuncture and Energy work as supports). As you can imagine this had a profound impact

One of those most significant experiences was a day where the sac around my heart, for an unknown reason, filled with fluid. A specialist was called from an hour away to empty that fluid, it was such an emergency that my husband was needed to assist. Despite this and despite the fact that this was the most painful procedure of the many I endured, it was one of the most peaceful and joy filled days in the entire event. Strangely, a few days later, on what was supposed to be a celebratory day, the day we harvested stem cells, I was overwhelmed with anger, sadness and frustration. These alternating days left me with a burning question, is our experience dependent on outside events? Since I had experienced otherwise, how did that happen? Could the grace I experienced that day become a stable way of being? Could I be in joy and peace no matter what is happening? This led to a full 12 years of intense search, reading, learning. My head is an active place, a place where I have planted a lot of seeds, cluttering it with ideas from all over science, metaphysics, religion, spirituality and psychology. The idea's started to converge into an awareness that the truth was inside of me, and in fact inside of all of us. In this book I will share the framework for relationships that has come to me and is helping me to stabilize in a state of Grace.

This information started coming in after what I thought were incessant referrals to "Karpmans Triangle". My dear friend Ria Meronek, a psychologist who loves positive psychology would relate stories of this work and how it influenced her practice and I would think "wow, she really likes this triangle thing".

Dr. Stephen B. Karpman M.D. envisioned the Drama Triangle in the 1960's. What started out as a sports play simplification became part of the foundation for the field of psychology and reiterations of the triangle and its application are bountiful.

Please check out Dr. Karpman's website www.KarpmanDramaTriangle.com for more information and access to his 2014 book A Game Free Life.

This information coupled with the belief that the answers are inside of me. In my search for inner answers I found myself in meditation in the home of transformational author, yoga instructor and meditation teacher Christine Wushke ((http://freelyhuman.com). Christine, in her humble way led a group of us into a deep meditation and allowed the space.

What unfolded for me was an experience of the triangle, point by point, similar in imagery to the 'Passion of the Christ' movie whipping scene but with arms outreached. My awareness moved from victim, to the 'punisher' and then to the crowd. It was in a non-pain, non-judgmental manner, just noticing and when fully felt, moving on to the next position. My question in the meditation was "what do we do then, how do we stop this?" This book is the answer that has emerged.

If you don't know that you have choices, then how do you choose? In this book I'm suggesting that point of view can be chosen. How you see the world makes an incredible difference in how you experience the world and how you react to it. Your world will reinforce what you believe. If beliefs are in your ability to change, then you can actually learn to enjoy this world, your life, no matter what!

Ultimately I would like to see us all having fantastic relationships. I want to live in a world where people get along and enjoy their lives. I believe that we have the maturity, connection and a growing will to actually make this happen on Earth. I am happy to be alive in these times and I want to support people in our world to be themselves and feel cared for and supported. Let's move from drama to trust, from hostile to harmonious.

Chapter One
The Drama Triangle

Do you ever feel like your life is made up of the same stories playing over and over? Different times, different faces with the same plot? We live in a world of drama, emphasized in our reality television, movies and even the news. We love stories, and whether we know it or not we are always telling ourselves stories. The stories we unconsciously tell ourselves have an impact on how enjoyable our lives are. Some of the stories we most like to tell are about relationships; love stories, villain and victims, battle stories. At their foundations they are: 'who am I to you and who are you to me'. In other words, how we relate to one another.

Relationships are a major factor in our wellbeing. "Healthy relationships are a vital component of health and wellbeing. There is compelling evidence that strong relationships contribute to a long, healthy, and happy life. Conversely, the health risks from being alone or isolated in one's life are comparable to the risks associated with cigarette smoking, blood pressure, and obesity." *Mary Jo Kreitzer, RN, PhD* We all sense this but too often feel powerless to make significant changes, this is because most of what we are doing is unconscious. Many workshop facilitators use the iceberg metaphor for this, the amount we are conscious of amounts to the tip of the iceberg with the larger part resting out of sight. Without awareness we repeat dysfunctional patterns, using the only tools that we have, even if they don't work!

Our personal relationships are seemingly shaped by a complex set of factors that include culture, society, parent-child interaction, upbringing, personality and experiences. No matter how you got where you are today, you can decide to now be the captain of the ship as you go forward. At the same time we need to take compassion along as our First Mate, we may have been travelling the same paths for a long time and retraining will take some focus.

Let's identify where we are now, what is working and what is not working and what we can do about it, let's make it simple.

In the 1960's Dr. Stephen Karpman developed a tool that represented the games we play in relationships. I've adapted Dr. Karpman's word 'Persecutor' to Bully as most of my work is school based and this is such a popular topic in our present culture.

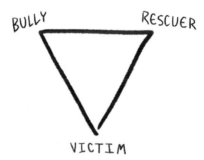

Drama Triangle, Dr. Stephen Karpman MD (**Persecutor adapted to Bully)

This outlines the interplay that happens in relationships, particularly when things are stressed or dysfunctional. Dr. Karpman's initial work was based on relationships between people. We will explore how we can apply this same framework to our inner life and to our association to other objects and situations in our lives (money, home, food, the body).

What I'm suggesting is that these are not 'who you are' but that they are points of view, costumes that you wear that form the terrain that you see. It is an orientation, and the Drama Triangle perspectives emphasize that there is a problem to be solved and someone/something is at fault. Take a step back and think about how often 'who did this and whose fault is this?' is our initial reaction.

Describing is helpful for understanding, but taking it the next step and finding our way to healthy relationships is where we want to go. To get to our destination it's helpful to understand where we are at; where we have been for a long time. We are going to explore each vantage point, its value and downfall. When we have full understanding we can make an informed choice. You could actually become the king or queen of your kingdom.

The following is a graphic representation of how I have come to understand the Drama Triangle and the private logic of the positions. The Circle of Trust encapsulates the triangle. When I am presenting this I see this in 3 dimensions, with the Triangle walls being vertical and therefore impairing the ability to see parts of the circle. The Drama is ensuing because a piece is blocked from sight. It is a challenge to represent in a stationary 2-dimensional manner so we will need to engage the imagination and I ask you to really step into the points of view. Embody them and imagine yourself in the spaces on the diagram. In this way we are not only building knowledge, but compassion and empathy as well (essentials to healthy relationship).

There is a second page with the triangle on it on the following page, feel free to rip it out of the book and use as we move through the book.

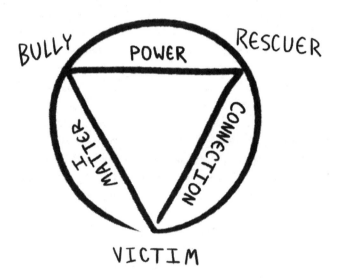

Tear Out

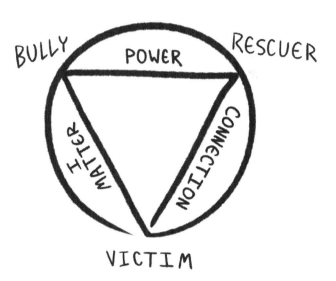

Notes:

Victim

We are going to start our spin around the Drama Triangle in Victim. A place where nobody plans to visit, but we all make trips here and more regularly than we think. A more empowering way to think of victim is 'taking a rest'. Sometimes this is a forced rest as in cancer victim, or any other physical ailment. Often this comes at a time when the world has become too big or too heavy for us and we 'check out' and look to others to own the power for a while. This presents the inner conflict of opening to being powerless in order to be helped and at the same time leaving yourself vulnerable to perceived attack.

In Victim other people, things and experiences fall into two broad categories, does this hurt me or does this help me? If we picture ourselves in this spot (using the diagram) we have 'I matter' and 'connected' in sight but the wall prevents us from seeing 'power'. So we know that we have some value here and that we have a connection to other people or things, but we can't see our ability to change anything. This might seem confusing as when we are in victim it can be because we don't have good self-esteem, but when we separate the 'I matter' from power it is more of an 'I matter' in my helplessness. So, the victim matters to the Bully because it is an affirmation of power and matters to the Rescuer because it gives them someone to save.

How do we feel here? Helpless, frozen, and waiting for circumstances to change and not feeling like there's anything you can do. Often times this is a default position. When the power or responsibility, gets to be too much, under the weight of too much work, or pressure, or burden we collapse into Victim with a "what about me?" "Who's going to help me?" "I tried but I can't".

"There is nothing I can do" The Victim tends to be voice-less as voice is power and as soon as you use it, "save me", you've reconnected with power and have the potential to shift perception.

As with all of the spots on the Drama Triangle, the Victim place is not all bad; the lack of responsibility is the curse and the value of this position. The power and there-fore the liability are not in your hands. If the power is out-side of you then you cannot be blamed, if you cannot be blamed, you remain innocent and outside of punishment! Or the punishment you are experiencing is unfair, which elicits greater sympathy. Underlying these thoughts are be-liefs, beliefs are down in the part of the iceberg that is sub-merged. A belief that given the power or the responsibility we would mess things up. There is a lack of faith here; faith and fear reside outside in other people or things. In Victim there is a secret belief that you cannot trust yourself, if you were trusted you'd mess up.

A great example of how this doesn't always have to be only about relationships with people is how we see money. In North American culture we have given money a lot of power, consider the thoughts "If I won the lottery I'd be free", or "I'm sad because I'm broke". Money be-comes Rescuer or Bully and we are left in a powerless po-sition with the thought "I can't" or "it's never enough". Our freedom or lack of it is often based in money and free-dom and power are closely linked. As a Victim of money we see ourselves in a powerless position, waiting for some outside change to save us.

The thoughts that run through our heads in Victim might be "I don't know what to do?" "If only _____ then I could _____". Our power is conditional on some other situation or person than pres-ently exists.

Oftentimes people in Bully or in Rescuer position will clearly see that the person HAS power that they are not using- remember the idea of powerlessness is a perception not a truth, the Victim is unconsciously choosing to see a wall where there is no wall. The walls are beliefs being projected out into the world and they seem very real. From the outside someone in another position may use phrase "why don't they just get a job?" Unconscious beliefs are keeping our Victim self from seeing what might be completely obvious to others. The other thing that we can often see when someone else is in Victim is that they have put themselves in this position and now they are complaining about it as if they had nothing to do with it. It can be frustrating from other viewpoints where power is so obvious. Frustration is not a good feeling, so when we are judging those in Victim, it's important that you remember that you would not be seeing someone in Victim if you were not also hanging out on the Drama Triangle! The effort used in judging could be more helpful in shifting into a healthy relationship spot instead. Part of getting out of the Drama Triangle is trading all judgment for curiosity, "what is keeping that person from seeing their own power or responsibility in this situation?" "What am I not seeing?"

We tend not to hold onto anything if it does not have some value; each of the Drama Triangle spots has an apex- a high point. The highest payoff for the victim viewpoint is absolute freedom from responsibility. In those rare moments when you are able to feel ahhh, the relief, without a question of a doubt that 'it' whatever 'it' was, was not in any way your fault and you have a momentary reprieve from the shame that we all lug around. That is a peak feeling; a moment of complete innocence. No matter what point you are at right now, just imagine the freedom of zero responsibility. As happens with any apex, it is temporary, a slippery slope and the fact that it's not real means that you can't stay there. Despite this, it is as good as we can imagine here and so we continue in the blind pursuit. I need to qualify that I believe we are in fact completely innocent, the innocence on the drama triangle is different from this true innocence in that it means someone else is at fault. Someone else is responsible. Fault is a driver on the drama triangle, what I know is that any story if seen from its entirety would be understandable. It's a matter of knowing the whole story, and we generally don't. It's like trying to understand a tapestry while looking at it through a microscope. It takes stepping back and taking it all in to see the greater organization and to make sense of the perfection of it. The view of the drama triangle is taking a slice out of that perfection and trying to reconcile it.

Our culture is heavily based on the Drama Triangle and so culturally you will find that we disempower based on gender, race, ability, sexuality and age. These societal norms are helpful to look at and perhaps question when we want to move to a healthier vantage point. Remembering that blame and shame are on the sideline so that we can clearly look at where we are at, this will help us to move from being reactive to being responsive. Consider the influence that who you believe you are and where you are in relation to each other affects how you see the world. Victimhood is contextual, not absolute, so statements like "he is such a victim" are less useful than "I am acting like a victim in this situation". We are all playing this somewhere and until we fully embrace ideals such as equality and inherent value, victimhood will continue. Awareness is the first step.

A Victim Case Story:

They often say that the first year of marriage is the hardest. One particular story that played out for Dusty and I was 'me at home and him out on the town'. This really hit high gear in terms of my victim viewpoint when we had kids (even now I can feel myself wanting to justify this position). Before kids I would lament that I couldn't go out because I had to work. After Jake was born it jumped to a long diatribe that went like this: "Here I am home with the baby and he is out with his good buddy Jody, he likes Jody more than me, he doesn't even want to come home, he doesn't even like me anymore" and then "this is so unfair, I'm stuck here all day alone with the baby and now all night, he doesn't even do anything, I never get to go out" I would imagine them out having the greatest time ever, while I was stuck at home. I would alternate between raging and crying. I would tell my story to girlfriends and they would agree that it was an outrage, that he was insensitive, that all men are like that, that men are selfish by nature. You would think that Dusty would come home and get a big lecture, but my comfort zone is rescuer to victim- so I would give him the silent treatment. He definitely knew I was angry but I wouldn't talk about it. We laugh about it now, he was actually relieved when he would ask "is something wrong?" and I would bark "no", he would think "phew, I'm off the hook". Luckily someone who I trust wouldn't stand for it. My Mom finally said "do you know where he is?" I did. He was at the Longview Bar and it was always on Fridays after hockey. "This is completely predictable, if you want to go out get a babysitter and meet him there." Yikes, could it really be that easy? The funny part is that I did it once, sitting there listening to two hours of hockey stories had me pining to be back home with my baby! It was not the story I had been telling myself at all, in fact part of the reason I married this guy was because he is fun and in the moment- exactly what I was trying to force out of him now and behavior that I was taking profoundly personally. As time went by I even had the courage to tell him about how I felt when he was out, he had no idea! In fact he assumed I was sleeping and wasn't calling because he didn't want me to wake up. These days he still goes out for drinks with the boys after hockey, I relax, I get the remote and watch whatever I want on TV OR I join them when I feel like it, I moved from victim to me.

Bully

Bullying is a hot topic in North America, we've moved from "boys will be boys" and "girls are mean" to a "we will not tolerate bullying" in schools and workplaces but definitely not in all arena's. Bullying remains a mainstay perhaps subtle, perhaps not, in politics, relationships, parenting, in corporations and in the media. Research on anti-bullying programs and their impact are not showing great results. I believe this is due to the same thing mentioned above, that it is contextual, someone is not a Bully, bullying is a behavior and the behavior is meaningful and useful or it would not be occurring. The reasons behind bullying behaviors once again are under the surface and are largely not being addressed. We Band-Aid the effect without getting at the cause. Despite what we have heard about "survival of the fittest" I believe that bullying is not human nature but an unnatural reaction based on misperception.

From the Bully point of view we have lost sight of connection. Using the diagram, we can see that when we stand in Bully we see power and we see that we matter and because of that wall- we are on our own. The best I ever heard this described was by Myles Himmelreich www.myleshimmelreich.com , an inspirational speaker who talks about living with Fetal Alcohol Effects. Miles says "if you were a baby and every time you were picked up you were dropped you would eventually stop asking to be picked up". From the Bully point of view there is a belief that people will let you down, it is valuable to be guarded and to avoid connection to other people. If you open up you will only get hurt or you will hurt them. Lack of connection is tied to guilt and although the Bully often hides it behind bravado there is usually a piece of them that has disconnected because they believe deep down that they are bad and that other people will find out and punish them. You can see how this unconscious fear (or belief) drives this to happen. As a comfort to this belief there will be some bluster overlay, the need to state 'awesomeness', bragging, pushing idea's, ramming an agenda to force our 'rightness' in the unconscious drive to prove our secret badness false or to hide it so that no one will know and we can avoid being punished.

When we are in Bully we can't afford empathy. Victims are seen as a means to prove our value, which is the connection to power. In Bully we often come into conflict with Rescuers because they are competing for power, for who is in charge. North American (and probably the world) culture is ruled by bullies, in the positive I call them catalysts, people who have power and believe that they matter. This will make more sense when we look at the healthy version of this viewpoint. Where you will often see this is with politicians, initially they are seen as support to the people and when they lose touch they are seen as bullies.

The peak experience from Bully comes from making it to the top on our own. The payoff is being the victor, the winner, all powerful. Our competitive society feeds on and rewards this. When we look at the origin of the word competitive it means to strive together, this definition would lead us to seeing each other as complementary to our own power rather than threatening to it. This is evidenced in things like the 4 minute mile, originally thought unattainable, once it was achieved it has become more regular. In this way when we push ourselves to be our best, and especially if coupled with natural ability, we open the doors for everyone.

In schools I have seen how this works against teachers, when in the Drama Triangle our response to bully's is either to try and over-bully (power trip), to rescue- which is rejected because it would require going to victim "I don't need you!! I don't need counselling" or to relate from victim. When adults relate to children from Victim (when the children have the power) this is not empowering it is scary. Kids know that there are things they can't do as kids and when the adults around them give out an 'I can't' they are left without support. This often engenders a disrespect from these children or youth "oh, you are a loser". What is needed is connection and support. This can be difficult to offer in the face of disrespect and refusal to be helped. It requires a lens switch to seeing scared instead of bad, seeing a cry for help as opposed to poor behavior. As I said, this does not mean that you disregard the behavior if it is anti-social, but you don't get emotional about it. You don't add shame or disconnect (expulsion, separation). You connect, "you seem like you could use some help right now", it's important to deal directly and as an adult about the behavior and at the same time allow this person some power- for example, you can't stand on your desk, you need to get down, would you like to cool down here or outside. Offering a choice instead of using a demand- while holding on to the expectation of positive behavior- allows power to be shared. Finding ways to connect with these kids when they are not elevated is crucial (this is not different for adults), showing genuine interest in them and what they like, and making opportunities to spend time together. Often I will hear adults say "they are just trying to get attention". Yes, this is true- so why wouldn't we give it to them? I'd rather give it to them playing one on one basketball than having to lecture them in an office. Using the Drama Triangle you can see the issue hiding behind the behavior. Instead of attending to the engine light you are opening the hood and seeing what is really wrong.

Connection is belonging. A Bully usually feels like they don't belong and they may take measures to demonstrate this by dressing different, or better, than everyone else, by not following the rules and by disrespecting authority. Even if we can see belonging from another aspect, remember that they can't see it, they question it, and in the Drama Triangle letting go of one viewpoint means taking another. So gaining connection can mean either going into victim-losing your power, or going into rescuer, losing your inherent value, this is the psychological difficulty when there is not a healthy option. Sometimes we see bullies banding together (gangs) to achieve that sense of belonging and therefore safety. It is innate to us as humans to hunger for belonging and to thrive when it is present. Belonging is a protective factor.

The feelings in Bully are guarded, on alert, primed, tense, expectant or ready for attack. There is usually anger when we are in Bully, disappointment or a sense of rejection. Anger can be a guardian of sadness and you will find that Bullies were sad before they were mad. Gangs work because they give bullies a place to feel understood and to not be all alone. The irony is that gangs have as much hierarchy and as many rules as the schools and society that gang members reject.

Other words for bully are as Karpman uses persecutor, punisher, aggressor or in a more positive light catalyst or 'mover and shaker; this is the system busting place to be and bullies tend to shake up our systems and break us from control.

Bully Case Story

As a mom I enter Bully when I have rescued for too long. I will finally snap and move over with my power to Bully and add some 'I matter'. It usually sounds like this "THAT'S IT, I've had it", it may have some berating "you are all so selfish", some door slamming and storming off. I will lose connection with how it is affecting the other, or maybe even purposefully hurt the other with a verbal attack (I'm not into to physical outbursts but throwing stuff and hitting shows up here). "I'M DONE" will come out of my mouth. So much of our own parenting was done this way that it can be shocking to us counsellor types who, though we know it's not helpful, will hear those words in our heads "quit crying or I'll give you something to cry about".

People who've grown up with a consistent Bully parent (or older sibling) will generally take this on, seeing that it's better to be the Bully than the Victim. This is a survival skill in a hostile environment and over time people lose the ability to even sense safety when it is there. They live perpetually 'on guard'. You can see how this can provoke the very situations they are trying to avoid (but expecting) to happen. Bully is a lonely place. It is the place where it's obvious that the Drama Triangle reinforces itself. Acting out of this lonely place with fear and anger leads to more aloneness, more fear, more guilt and more anger.

Rescuer

Rescuer is a corner where you see your power and you see connection. Unfortunately, you can't see that you matter. Everyone else matters but your value is dependent on rescuing. If there is a problem, we can fix it, in this space we are the helper. We glorify this position, the 'martyr', people who give their all, people who give without asking, the good girl and selfless guy.

Rescuers have a difficult time receiving. If your meaning and merit are tied to helping it's hard to accept being on the other side. "I'm fine" becomes your mantra.

The ultimate experience for the Rescuer is when you actually save someone; you are the exalted hero, the saviour. In rescuer you are vigilant for people in need and often drop your own needs when others needs come up. Self- care, although often recognized as important, seems to never leave the bottom of the list.

In Rescuer you are connected to the pain of the world and you feel a fire to make the world a better place. It can be exhausting and frustrating. By keeping all of the responsibility (you need it to feel valuable) the people you are helping, the Victims, cannot make change without you, a classic co-dependent relationship.

The power that the Bully and the Rescuer seem to share looks a little different from each perspective. "I can" without connection looks like power with a capital P, whereas "I can" with connection looks like responsibility. Rescuers are going to save the world and Bullies are going to take it over. Both have confidence and both require Victims to assert the position, in this way the powerless are needed and valuable! Although we find places that are more comfortable for us, we usually slide along one line or another, these are NOT who we are and are simply ways of seeing the world. Because they are not truth and not the whole story they are not stable. Something is always missing. Something is always missing, have you noticed that feeling? It is a primary motivator of so much of our behavior, seeking and seeking for that thing outside of us. This is draining and means that eventually the Rescuer will move into Bully, with a stomp and a door slam to disconnect, or into Victim in tears of "what about me?" in the bathroom where no one can hear. The corresponding guilt associated with this move reinforces the system and keeps it going.

Rescuers often have a look about them, that even if they told you that they value themselves, you will see that they don't take care of their physical appearance, or home or vehicle, they may be overweight. It's a function of quickly eating what's available as they run around saving the world and never giving themselves the time that proper diet, nutrition and sleep afford. In rescuer your value comes from being needed, without that you feel lost and useless.

Rescuer Case Story

In my private practice my tagline is "helping helpers" so I see a lot of Rescuers. As I've stated before, the primary one stares at me in the mirror most mornings. My favorite story of being in Rescue mode is when my children were first in school. I spent hours at that school, I ran the breakfast program, I photocopied, I read, and the pinnacle was singlehandedly organizing, decorating and working the Grandmothers tea by myself!!! At the same time I was exhausted, my house was in shambles and like many volunteers I was growing resentful and growly at the other Mom's. I was also the crisis counsellor at the Boys Ranch and a willing ear for anyone with a problem near or far. I'm not saying that I was doing poor work, but truthfully how much responsiveness could I have? I was consistently stressed about my house and any comment whatsoever about the state of the house would shoot me quickly into Bully mode! The signs of Rescuer here are the lack of care for my own things, the resentment, the defensiveness and the fatigue- not sustainable and all fueled by the drive to be appreciated and 'worthy'. This drive was not in my awareness, I just thought I was super helpful. I was busy being a good girl, good wife, good friend, and good mom.

Overview

We take turns moving around the triangle, building patterns of relationship. These can be contextual, Bully with one friend, Victim to another. In times of real stress we may find ourselves particularly confused, spinning round and round. That feeling is intense. When you can't find your grounding, when you cry (Victim) and then gnash your teeth (Bully) and then try to bargain (Rescuer) as can happen when we have a death of a family member, job loss or any other situation that we haven't already conditioned ourselves to be in. Let me be clear that there is nothing wrong here; it's just what is and how we have been relating for millennia. My suggestion is that we can rise above these roles and mature into a healthier place. We need to have compassion for the Drama Triangle, it is not driven by 'bad' it is driven by scared. We respond differently to scared people than we do to perceived 'bad' people.

	Belief	Thought	Feeling	Behavior
Victim	I Can't	There's nothing I can do. If only… Worlds against me Someone help.	Helpless Expectant Persecuted Less than Afraid	Complaining Waiting Making excuses Passive.
Bully	I'm On My Own	I need to watch my back They are out to get me I decide Nobody understands	Vigilant, Tense On edge Unsupported Critical Afraid.	Bravado Aggressive Defensive Dynamic Antisocial
Rescuer	I Have To Help	I need to do something Those poor people This is not good I can solve it I know how they feel and I'm going to do something about this	Self-righteous Hopeful and occasionally frustrated Guilty (too much) Sympathy	Busy helping Dropping balls in other areas e.g. Care of own family and self-care. Reliable Everyone knows they can count on them to pitch in

The Outsider and Grace

As I was saying at the beginning of this chapter I see the model 3 dimensional; so picture this down at the bottom of the orb. When someone 'let's go' of more than one vantage point they slip down into a dark place where they do not see connection, do not see their value and do not see their power. This is like falling into the depths, where we move from shadows to the dark night. From how it's been described to me this would be depression, a space that's beneath the triangle where the not secure identity is lost, where separation from self and from community leaves a person feeling hopeless, worthless, lost, alone and unable to do anything about it. In this place you neither want to help, to hurt or to be helped, you become immobilized.

If you visualize two tetrahedrons (two triangles in 3D) inside an orb, one tetrahedron is our Drama Triangle with a three dimensional point, rock bottom you might say is what I'm calling "the Outsider" a keenly painful point to be at, a point that can be transformative or result in the end of the personal story all together. From this point we would see entering into bully, rescuer or victim as a move up or a healing.

The other triangle in the orb representing the Healed Triangle and its point, a point at which you can see all of the picture, a pinnacle, I am calling Grace. A state of Grace where you can see that you are powerful, that you are connected and that you are valuable. This is a place where you rise above the drama and are able to see the story with more clarity. From here you can extend understanding to yourself and to the other players in the game. You can feel the draw or temptation of the points but you have the ability, and make the choice to resist this temptation, refusing to take a limited point of view.

The Big Issue

The problem with living out from the Drama Triangle is that no point is sustainable. There is always a piece missing and we have this vague awareness that something is missing, it is stressful and depleting. Often our most comfortable places in the Drama Triangle can be traced back to a childhood experience. When we listen to our thoughts we can hear recurring stories. One of my spiritual teachers, Nouk Sanchez, reminds us "None of us has been raised by an Ascended Master yet". Due to its inherent instability we can only stay in one position for so long and eventually we will move out and into another spot. For example in Rescuer we will help and help, unfortunately, since I'm holding all the power, the helpless may not get better, in which case I will eventually throw my hands up and disconnect- moving directly over to Bully "fine then, if you aren't going to help yourself I'm done with you" or move into Victim "I try and I try but nothing ever changes, there's nothing I can do, when do I get someone to care about me?" Holding the full burden of responsibility – whether for yourself (Bully) or others (Rescuer) becomes heavy and eventually a collapse will happen and you will rest in Victim a while.

I myself, tend to find Rescuer most comfortable and when challenged generally move down into Victim. I really value connection so rarely do I move into Bully with other people. However, I've uncovered a healthy inner bully who is happy to point out my faults and whip me rather incessantly!

In this reading I invite you to personalize the information, where do you feel comfortable? Are there any of these definitions having you say "I do that" I've noticed we have a tendency to identify how other people fit in the triangle, this is helpful to deepen the learning but remember

If you notice someone else on the Drama triangle, you are there, how are they relating to you? If you see a Bully, are you a Victim of that person, a Rescuer or are you being called to overpower and therefore become the Bully yourself? We set blame and shame aside, this activity is not to induce fear or guilt but to name where you are or feel most comfortable. The truth is that none of the points of view on the Drama Triangle feel 'good'. There is a fear element at play. In fear we as humans have a biological response, 'fight or flight'. Rescuer and Bully are fight responses, Bully may be violent or aggressive acts as they are not connected.

The back story of the Drama Triangle is that there is something missing, a mistake, somethings gone wrong and it's someone's fault. All guilt requires punishment and so this becomes a self-actualizing and reinforcing system where we are perpetually stressed and in survival mode. Whether that threat is real or perceived, our brains and nervous system react the same. We are now finding out that our physical body does not respond well to this consistent state of danger and stress and it's proving to be a reliable predictor of future physical and mental health issues.

What the Drama Triangle often ends up with is an internal battle that feels terrible, the question of "do I choose my heart?" Or "do I choose their heart?" in other words be selfish (Bully and Victim) or be selfless (Rescuer). This is not a win-lose situation it is lose-lose. We are an ecosystem of humanity and how we feel, act and be together affects the whole, which includes yourself. I may choose to be selfish but there will be a price to pay for it. In this case the price would be disconnection or loss of power, or I could choose to be selfless and I lose my value outside of the selflessness. Keep in mind that this is a perception, in truth- if we were all to look after ourselves - imagine how that would help the whole of us.

Are we doomed to this reactive and well entrenched story line? I am going to suggest not. With awareness, mindful approaches to relationships, and a willingness to acknowledge and choose another mindset, we can find ways that allow us to sustain well-being and consistent access to our inherent and unconditional value, connection and power.

Chapter Two
Circle of Trust

When we begin to recognize our stories it can bring a mix of 'wow, I understand' and 'oh, no! I didn't realize' we are so entrained to the drama that blame and shame quickly creep in. So this is another reminder that we are setting the concept of blame and shame aside. You are welcome to pick them back up when you are not reading. I think of them like Thing One and Thing Two in the Cat and The Hat story; they facilitate confusion and cause chaos. In plain speak what I'm saying is that if you notice that you are in Victim, in Bully or in Rescuer please do not feel bad about it!!! Do not be a Bully to yourself. Notice your position and with a light hearted' oops' make another choice. The other choice is where we are going now.

So let's imagine that we could move from the Drama Triangle into that point of Grace see from a point of healthy relationship. What would that even look like? What would it look like to stop playing role after role? Watching hopeful relationships crash up against a wall, experiencing disappointment after disappointment. Imagine a drama free life. There is a feeling of dread that comes with drama, waiting for the other shoe to drop. Sometimes even to the point that we swear off relationship and cut people out entirely. There is hope. There is a way and I've used it in my personal life, in a work setting and as a leader. I'm happy to walk along side of you as we grow up, evolve relationships and consciously create not only healthy relationships but a better world.

How we relate to things is based on how we see ourselves and how we see others. Perception has a profound effect on relationships and perception is relative to our inner and outer stories. In moving from a dysfunctional relationship, the Drama Triangle, to a healthy relationship we must shift both how we see ourselves and how we see others. Identity informs relationship. Who I believe I am will affect how I act with and towards other people and who I think they are. Up until now this has probably been an unconscious process colored by upbringing, personality and past experiences. The lens we see through is complex and until acknowledged and explored we see drama as a reality out of our control. There is great value in taking time to step back and take a look at our relationships, how we see ourselves in relation to other people, how we feel around others and how we behave. If it doesn't feel good the Drama Triangle gives you a framework to recognize where things might be going wrong and how your perceptions could be distorted. In this chapter we will explore the potential for healed relationship and how the Circle of Trust connects to the Drama Triangle.

When we take down the walls, taking out the triangle, we can have a more full and sustainable experience. We can respond to ourselves, others and our inner story instead of reacting to misperceptions or slivers of the real story. Each of the points on the Drama Triangle has a corresponding healed aspect.

Victim becomes Free Expression

Bully becomes Support

Rescuer becomes Care.

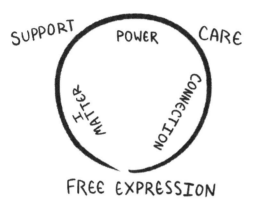

Free Expression

When you connect your Victim aspect to power you will get Free Expression. In other words, giving permission to be, to speak from where you are at, to get your story out in some way.   Another way to say Free Expression is to be yourself. You take that line that was a wall and you choose to see through it. "Even though I'm feeling powerless, believing myself powerless, I'm willing to look past this to the truth".

When we allow expression through words, pictures, dance, music, sport, etc. we reconnect to power, to our sense of "I can". This is a constructive use of the energy of emotion as opposed to a destructive use.

In my counseling and coaching work it has become obvious that the answer to anyone's problem lies right under that problem. Often I will find that when you hold the space (with care and support) for people to free express it goes like this:

Blah, blah, blah, blah, blah, blah, blah, blah, blah, blah, blah. (The story, which in some cases may be very long. compassionate and patient listening is a must.)

Stop. As a Rescuer this is the hard part. Resist jumping in with your awesome ideas.

Person Sighs. Shoulders drop, head nods.

"But you know…"

A SOLUTION

Not just a solution, but THEIR solution. Something in the victim logic is telling them that responsibility is NOT what they want, they've allowed that wall. Often this is a belief that they will "mess things up", they can't trust themselves to take power. They will be able to bring up evidence of when this has happened. The conversation usually moves from blame to shame to solution, blame and shame are not strong enough to withstand attention, but they feel bad enough that we avoid attending to them. It is like the bogeyman under the bed, the fear keeps you from looking, but once you do- nothing. There is a fear that the words behind the fear "you are not good enough, you will be punished, you don't matter" just might be true.

In North American culture this is reinforced early with language and messaging that tends to "whose fault is this?" Finding fault is generally the first course of action and in doing so decides who must be punished. Thankfully we are finding out that punishment does not work as a deterrent to bad behavior or as a motivator for good behavior and more often than not reinforces the issues already in play. For example disconnecting the bullies, kicking them out of school or putting them in detention centers or jail. Helping yourself or others to pull out of Victim stance will require patience. What is keeping you/them there is well entrenched and has served a need (the need to not be responsible).

Those of us who lean toward rescuing have to consciously stop ourselves from solving the problem, even if we have the greatest answer ever, and be mindful in our work to empower rather than build dependence. It can be a great feeling to have the answer to somebody's problem, but once you start, there will be people lining up for the answer and soon you will be overwhelmed!! Of course this doesn't mean you don't use your expertise. Doctors, counsellors or any other person who has knowledge and/or experience to support decisions is bound to do so. You need to check in that you are not putting that persons needs consistently above your own and that you are not holding all of the power and having all of the answers without their input. When you are truly in a victim space, a space where you're in danger, your free expression may come in the form of calling the police or going to a shelter, or screaming.

The most helpful you can be to move out of Victim space is to hold for yourself and for others the belief that the answer to any issue or problem is available and that the person with the seeming problem is key in finding that answer. This is a shared power, giving the Victim all of the power only shifts them to Bully or Rescuer. This is a lot of the messaging that we've learned to deal with bullies, at one time your parents would say "just deck them", shifting you from Victim to Bully! When we allow Victims to free express to bullies (as in Restorative Justice Circles) we give the bully an opportunity to see their impact and therefore connect with the victim. Sometimes, because they are disconnected, they don't even realize that they have affected their so called Victims. This is about understanding not guilt.

Free expression at its best is sharing you. You, at your essence, are here with purpose and promise and when that is shared it contributes to the wellness of the world.

Self-Expression Case Story

In my work in schools I had a girl who consistently came to our office crying, even in the hallway she regularly had red eyes and looked scared. This little girl saw herself as powerless in her middle school and often saw herself as bullied and needing the help of teachers. She had teachers who regularly walked her around the school with their arm around her. One day she showed up in my office, crying, and as luck would have it I had two other girls and a boy (Bullies) in the room with me. I asked her if she was okay with the other kids there and she said yes. Coming from Care and Support (Rescuer would have kicked those other girls out) I asked what was wrong and she said that she wanted to try out for the talent show but she was afraid people would make fun of her. She talked about all of the bad things that could happen, including feeling stupid, being laughed at, being embarrassed, forgetting her song. She had made the decision not to try out and now was just sad because she really liked singing, but couldn't see herself doing it. One of the other kids in the room was a talented musician and I asked him how he dealt with it, I asked if he had ever felt like this girl and he shared that until he tried it he felt like that all the time. We talked about the feelings that she was afraid of- which were exactly what she was already feeling!!!! Finally she brightened a little, taking some strength from looking at how limiting her own story was and the logic that it wasn't going away if she never tried. While we were talking the two girls made little posters that said "You can do it!" and "You've got this". She walked herself down to the music room and she auditioned, it wasn't perfect, she was stiff, but it surprised the music teacher in how great her voice was- nobody knew. I look forward to seeing how her story emerges from here.

Support

Bully to Support may be hard to believe, but I am shocked at the number of times I have believed myself a Victim of someone and when I voice my needs, wishes or discontent, these people turn out to be the biggest support. Even in the story above the 3 supposed 'bullies' in my counselling room were complete supportive to my sad little friend. Much like free expression allows the Victim to become Free Expression, the way to get the Bully to Support is **with** support. Even just changing your own viewpoint can change how you see that Bully in your life. I have now started asking myself- "is this person actually a support and I'm missing that?" Liking to have power myself I am often triggered by strong people that I feel might be trying to boss me. I don't like it. Since I've been asking myself this question I have found my own ability to collaborate and to make life easier on myself has increased and my perception that someone is trying to tell me what to do has diminished.

When using the framework you can ask "what is missing here?" From Bully you cannot see connection and you do not feel supported. Connecting and supporting and a dash of patience are required to shift ourselves or others out of Bully. The patience is necessary because there is a value to being in this position. The value being that you don't need to rely on others and therefore won't be let down. What we have on our side is that these are ONLY viewpoints and not the reality of who we are. Inside even the most hardened Bully is a Victim and a Rescuer. In truth all three parts are in play anytime we are in drama- which much of life has been so far. Remember support does not always need to be us. Recognizing that a spouse is a Bully may require you to get the support of friends, family or counselling.

These points of view are not stable, so there is never a lost cause; there is a truth in us that knows that connection is part of what we need. In fact science is now showing us just how crucial connection is to our survival. It has been known for a while that babies who are not held and interacted with will not thrive and recent studies are showing that community and positive relationships are a powerful factor in mental and physical health.

When we are in Bully we alienate and reinforce the belief that we are alone and people will let us down. Rescuers do not work well with bullies because they both want power, in order for a rescuer to work with a bully they sometimes attempt to shift them to victim.

In working with Child and Family Services I often saw this between social workers and families. When the social worker would see the parent as a 'bully' or 'bad guy' and likewise from the parent point of view and they both see the child as the victim they would have an incredibly hard time working together. The social worker would see their responsibility for taking care of the child, and you can see how we think "yes, that is right". The problem comes with the fact that we end up taking care of people's children when they, with some support and connection, may be very capable. Taking kids into care is traumatic for all involved and the statistics on returning home become poor after 6 months in care. This is fracturing to families and puts a large financial and moral burden on our system. Parents in these situations are naturally sad and angry, afraid and guilty and if they are in 'fight' response, which may have led to the problem in the first place, they will disconnect from the social worker who they are reliant on for the return of their children. You can see how this becomes a separation story, frustrating for all. How this would look practically are long stand-offs over who's going to make phone calls "Mom, needs to phone me to arrange the appointment" which doesn't help anyone. You may see this as giving the parents power, my experience is that to make things work we must share the power, this might mean making the phone call first, it always means meeting people where they are at and not where you would like them to be.

        This is quite a shocker to us in a professional sense, we have bought into the fact that we are doing good. We even reinforce the fact that some people just shouldn't have any power and therefore our prison system is bursting. The bully will tend towards power and the rescuer will tend towards responsibility, consider the relationship between governments and not for profit agencies. Often the government is perceived to have all of the power and the agencies they refer to have all of the responsibility. I have been more connected to agencies, I'm sure from the government side it looks the very opposite.

        A Bully who is connected becomes a Support. I will often use this knowledge with at-risk kids who are in a state of defiance, I will find a way for them to help me. I will quickly think of a job that lets them shine- particularly if it's lifting something as that has additional sensory calming qualities. In this way they keep power and connect, if they will not I will at least let them keep some decision making powers, as long as it is not a safety risk. This might be letting them choose where we are meeting or what we are doing, a shared power, not a giving over of power. As rescuers there are times when giving over our power can happen too and we demote ourselves to victim in order to avoid conflict. Bully position WANTS support, the fear is of a let-down. Staying in care and support and allowing Free Expression (maybe it's even a litany of curses initially until you build relationship and can ask for it otherwise) builds trust.   When someone is missing something, whether it is power, connection or their value, taking another piece away can feel like too much, nobody wants to be the Outsider. This is why Bully can escalate when power is attempted to be taken away or Victim can be distraught if we demean or disconnect from them. I have seen a lot of Rescuer wars in my work world, posturing over whom has the degrees or experience or position and therefore the ultimate power. This is usually veiled by smiles and high level language volleys, but the threat is still there and felt. The perception of having power or connection taken away from a Rescuer will certainly up the alarm and intensify fight or flight responses, potentially moving them over to bully or victim. The bottom line is that we are all connected and everyone needs and deserves support and care.

Support Case Story

Working in residential care for so many years you see bully after bully (this is how they were seen by others- not the truth) these kids had blown out of every school and foster care situation leaving them as candidates for residential care. Adult wary and tough on the outside, they were still little kids and still hungry for positive adult attention. Let down many times they would test your mettle, what some call attachment disorder seems like a logical consequence to being serially disappointed. An attitude of "I like you no matter what" coupled with "You can trust me to run the show" and clear boundaries and expectations would yield the most brilliant young men. One of the best ways I have heard of to describe the way to be with these kids was from a marketing expert (Tad Hargraves). In speaking about marketing/sales he described that we need to avoid being moved along a continuum that has aggressive on one end and collapsing on the other. He talked about how we talk about our pricing and if someone questions it we can tend to move over to "that's the price- take it or leave it" or pushy sales tactics or "oh, is that too much? What do you want to pay" and turn into mush. He suggested that we strive to get off of the continuum and stay composed- he used a dot to illustrate this. This is the price and I'm good with it no matter what your response.

Using this same type of holding your composure when working with youth (and in fact helpful in all relationships) would allow these kids to remain empowered and be eager to help! When the Town of High River flooded, as it has occasion too, our youth had the opportunity to shine. One year a team were needed for emergency sandbagging and they were lauded as 'heroes'. They worked tirelessly beside adults and even years after many recounted that event as pivotal in their development, the opportunity to help and to be seen as helpful.

Seeing the Canadian Forces drive into High River after the 2013 flood to help homeowners gave me such a warm feeling. These young people who genuinely want to help their country are often put in a position of 'bully' having to disconnect from the 'bad guys' and use their power and value against fellow human beings. In the case of High River they were able to use their skills and equipment to support the community with no need for sacrifice and therefore a graceful use of an `asset and an opportunity to be the support to Canadians that they signed up for.

Care

The healed Rescuer realizes that they too are valuable. Valuable for more than just how helpful they are, they will be willing to be helped even! I often visualize the Rescuer as the smiling person standing by the pool holding everyone's flip flops and sunscreen while everyone else plays in the pool. They will argue that they like it this way; they just want everyone else to be happy. Secretly they fear that they are valueless and their only worth is in helping others, in holding flip flops. As I said before this type of service is highly prized in our culture and people often try to shift children from Bully to Rescuer "why can't you just be helpful like your sister?" Often Rescuer is held in place by guilt. When your worth is so heavily reliant on helping, you assume that if you are needing something or receiving that there is a loss to someone else. Often these people are told- you have to stop doing so much for others, look after yourself! We must realize that while it gets tiring, helping others is feels good, we don't need to throw the baby out with the bath water. The title of Care means that you care not only for others but also for yourself. The reminder that I give to Rescuer is that I am not asking them to stop helping, I'm asking them to join the circle, jump in the pool! They are often very good at picking up on others needs and it may take a bit of practice to tune back into your own wishes, dreams and desires. I've had many, women in particular, say to me "I don't even know what I like" as they have spent a lifetime meeting the needs of others. As with the other points of view, Rescuer needs some faith that they are cared for to shift to Care. Outwardly acting as Rescuer there may be an active bully and victim on the inside. Namely the bully that tells you that you are not good enough and the victim who feels powerless to act on behalf of the self. Self-support and Self-expression through methods such as journaling, reflection, meditation and art are ways to get in touch with and move into Care.

Care Case Story

I was tossed into Care with the diagnosis of Cancer. After hanging out in Rescuer for so long it was incredibly difficult to accept help from family and friends, particularly in the care of my children. The reason the cancer got to a Stage IV was that I was too busy looking after everyone else to take time and demand an answer to a month's long illness. I persisted with my daily life despite weight loss, consistent flu like symptoms, lack of breath and exhaustion. Luckily I wasn't tossed into Victim perspective for very long; Grace was quick to find me and pick me up and was the impetus for all of this work. Not satisfied with doing this once, when I received my second cancer diagnosis 12 years later, and after doing this work for some time I was able to truly apply it consciously. I said 'yes' to every offer of help and continued with some of my own caring work at the same time. During the first event I realized helping as a core of my being when a night nurse turned to me in the wee hours of the morning (I was receiving a stem cell transplant and was rarely sleeping) and said "I saw on your chart that you are a counsellor, can I ask you a few questions about me and my boyfriend". It was a profound gift after being cancer victim identity for a few months. So the second time around I received help and gave help freely I was caring and cared for, supported and supportive and I was honest about my feelings. The first time around I cried alone in the bathroom and then complained in counselling that nobody understood how hard it was and I always had to be happy so that my family wouldn't be upset. Finally, I recognized that the value of cancer is the guilt free caring and that I needed to 'have the cancer goodness without the cancer'. I will now take 'cancer without the cancer' days, days where I stay in bed in my pajamas and let other people look after things, days when I will admit that I'm tired and admit that I don't want to help anymore. I allow my family to have their feelings and try not to be the chief emotional officer.

Moving from Rescuer to Care will take some compassion for yourself and some patience. When you start you will see the guilt and insecurities that have been holding you to saving the world. You may have situations arise that   highlight that you are really needed and that you are the only one who can help. This doesn't mean you stop that, you just check in first and see where you are coming from.

	Belief	Thought	Feeling	Behaving
Free Ex-pres-sion	It's okay to be me It's okay for us to be differ-ent and to ex-press our personal truths	I can be… I will cre-ate I can	Creative Free Empowered Seen Accepted Courageous Eager Able Confident	Freely speaking or expressing in some way Unique
Care	Every-body Matters	It's great to give and it's great to receive.	Tender Thoughtful Kind Empathic Valued Balanced Calm	Considerate of others, while at the same time considerate of self. Self-respectful and communi-cates own need and truth.
Sup-port	There's a way, we can do this.	I can help I'm useful	Capable, Confident Senses what needs to be done and how to do it Connected Solid Present	Helpful in a more physical way than care, offering physi-cal assistance, financial sup-port or 'back up'.

Recovering Outsider

If we feel worthless, powerless and disconnected and are truly in the dark this may be a time when compassionate power actually steps in to lift the person. Avoiding bullying and rescuing by using empathy and checking in with the person, even if they say "I don't want help" "go away" or "I don't care". This is a time where we care for them until they move into a place with some power, some worth or recognizing some connection. Empowering them by asking questions "who do you feel the most comfortable to help you" "can I come over, can I come with you" and keeping yourself and your own fear in check.

We are connected. Our biology proves it with 'mirror neurons', so it can be very hard to stay composed when dealing with someone who is believing themselves to be the Outsider. Regularly applying the skills in this book will help you to maintain Grace in spite of the words or actions of another and the more you do it the better you get at it. It requires not buying into the drama while maintaining empathy for the person who is.

Application

Now that I know this, what do I do? We are programmed to start at the doing. This is more about where your behaviors are coming from than the specific behaviors, at times the activity or behavior can be exactly the same for the Drama Triangle and the Circle of Trust. As an example let's use taking my Mom to a doctor's appointment. Let's consider two alternates, same outcome but the difference is the beliefs, thoughts and feelings behind the action. A clue that you are on the Drama Triangle when going on this trip is a **feeling** of resentment creeping in, usually followed by an inner reprimand and a dose of guilt.

It might go like this "Can you take me to my appointment on Tuesday", you had planned to have a day off with a massage but you quickly say yes, cancel it and take your mother. On the way there she mentions that your sister was asked first but she was busy, you feel some anger rise up.

Alternatively, from the Circle of Trust your mother asks you if you can take her, you explain what you were planning and your mother expresses that she's already asked everyone else, you tell her that you will take her if you can change your appointment, you establish whether or not she could change her appointment, in other words, you matter too. In the end you may end up just as before, going to the doctor and changing your plans, but in the second scenario it is a response to the whole picture and not an automated, or conditioned response based on obligation, requiring sacrifice and leaving you resentful!

Application requires action, you can have this knowledge, understand the points of view, talk about it, analyze it, etc. but at the end of the day it's only helpful if you use it.

Here is the signature story that exemplifies a time when I consciously used this framework to not only guide my inner sense of wellness but also to achieve a win- win outcome.

In 2011 I was working as the crisis counsellor at our family business. Our family business, the Stampede Ranch for Kids, was a residential group home based on a Ranch in Southern Alberta. We were home to over 1500 kids in our 38 year existence. The youth that lived with us were supported by Alberta Child and Family Services and came with multiple adverse childhood experiences resulting in behavioral issues.

On this day I was lounging at home after a busy week when I got a phone call from the manager telling me that Bobby (name changed) had been talking about killing himself and could I please come up and see him. My early morning relax quickly turned to angst and I found myself in a state of upset. I was pacing around the house and fuming. I had been spending a lot of time on the staying peaceful in spite of outer experiences so I caught myself and asked "what is going on?" Before going up I sat for a few moments and just noticed what I was thinking and feeling. It was a run around the triangle. **Victim** "why do I have to go up there? I never get a day off when I want one" **Bully** "the staff should be able to handle this, why the heck do we even train them on suicide intervention if they can't use it" "I shouldn't even go, I will tell them it's my day off and they can deal with it", notice the blame and lack of empathy for the fact that the staff had been dealing with this boy for days and were at the end of their knowledge and ability. **Rescuer** "oh my goodness, he's been really down, there is a real danger here, what if I do it wrong? He could really kill himself and I don't know if the staff will watch him good enough. Do I remember my suicide intervention training, should we just send him to the hospital?" I was afraid because this was not a kid that I knew well, so I questioned his connection to me. Round and round I was reeling. The loudest voice was the rescuer, so I said to myself "Okay, I see I am in rescuer, can I shift to Care and Support?" It was an instantaneous relief. Care is easy for me; I do it all the time. In that moment I connected with the fact I didn't have to do it all on my own, I drove up in a completely different state of mind.

That was great but what unfolded showed the value of coming from this different state of 'being'. So being care and support I found Bobby at school. He was sitting at his desk with his head down on his arms and looking shut down. I tapped him on the shoulder and said "hey, Joel called me and told me you had a bad morning, do you want to come with me?" He said "NO". If I had been in Rescuer

I would have demanded he leave with me, potentially even shifting to Bully and having him forcibly removed 'for his own good'. I was coming from Care and Support so I pulled up a chair and looked at what he had in front of him. He started talking, Free Expressing, he talked about how stupid he was "I'm 14 and I can't even read" His teacher, also in the room and obviously flustered to have me there quickly came over and showed me what he'd been working on and how far he'd come. I communicated that it was all good (also care and support for teacher) and I was just going to listen for a bit. I mentioned to the boy that the other students could potentially hear him and maybe he'd like to speak privately, again he said "NO" I could have seen this as defiance, but what I saw was a need to keep some power, and really I was happy to share power with him, he chose to stay and I chose to stay with him. As opposed to me going into Victim and just leaving "I tried and he won't talk to me". He continued to talk about how much school he'd missed and how he was probably just going to be a drunk like all of his uncles and so what was the point of school or living or anything. He continued on and on, venting frustration and letting his thoughts out, I listened actively. Eventually he stopped, he paused, he took that big breath and he said "Or, I could be like Darryl". Darryl was one of our staff, also First Nations, a calm, quiet and strong man. He was well liked by all of our youth and an excellent role model. I said "Yes, there's no reason you couldn't be like Darryl, do you connect with him?", "Yes, he said, I really like him". Then he said "How long do I have to talk to you". I laughed and said "It's up to you, how are you feeling? Are you still having thoughts of killing yourself?" He said he was feeling fine and wanted to finish his work, I thanked him and asked if I could share a bit with Darryl so that he knew what was going on, he said yes. I then left and alerted the staff to keep a close eye on him, what we called

24 hour supervision, continuing to take his previous sui-
cidal thoughts seriously but not assessing him to need a trip
to the hospital. As I came away I was light and I could tell
that he was lighter too, we had a plan and it was one that
worked for both of us and his risk of hurting himself was
lowered.

If I had gone in with my professional hat firmly in
place my training would have told me that I had to speak
with him in a private space that he had to listen to my as-
sessment and answer my questions. It's not hard to imagine
how that may have played out. By sharing power with him
we were able to build some trust, he was able to speak because he felt safe in the familiarity of his classroom and the
teacher in a bit of overhearing was able to build some empathy for a student who he had previously believed did not
care about his work. I had made sure that the conversation
was at a low volume and other boys were busy with other
projects and were not affected, although in them seeing the
conversation, the fact that I was someone they could talk
to was reinforced and demystified.

I am not at all saying that you should do your counselling in a classroom, the prescription is not in the action,
but in where I was coming from and how I was seeing him.
I was able to respond to the situation instead of reacting or
following a pre-determined script. I could have seen him
as Bully but I saw someone who needed support, someone
who needed to keep his power and it was up to me to connect with him. It was valuable for my own wellbeing to see
that even though I had the greatest level of education in
the program I was not everything. He was not my responsibility alone and I could share the care of this boy with
Darryl, the teacher and the other staff. I could return to my
day off knowing that he was probably going to be okay and
I could relax. In my Rescuer zone I would often stay late
and take home worry, micromanage staff and create rules

and limitations in order to have the illusion of control, this would have been counterproductive with the kids that we had in our home.

Contrary to what you might think, a healthy relationship only requires one person. One person in Grace can shift a situation and that person will have the freedom and ability to leave that situation without the need to cause harm to themselves or others.

For example let's consider a truly abusive husband/wife; let's say the one who is being abused identifies that they have been coming from Victim in their relationship. Free Expression to the abuser would be great and would require courage, and may or may not be possible; I would never encourage someone to put themselves in danger. Free Expression to yourself by journaling, meditation or inner conversations may reveal some insight that allows a shift from this position and a connection to power. For example, in reflection you might discover a belief that if you resist or tell the truth to this person you will lose them and never have anyone to love again, generally there will be some kind of inner story that is keeping the position in place. Once you see these beliefs it is so much easier to question them. Uncovering that you deep down believe that you somehow deserve it or that it's your fault let's your brain start to ask questions and find solutions, while this is hidden you seem stuck. If it feels too dangerous to speak with the person you are with that is a sign that you need other players in the mix. Free Expression to an outside source can also serve to illuminate your own part in accepting Victim as a position and potentially, with help, inspire movement from this place.

Opening up from the Drama Triangle to the Circle of Trust and moving into Care, Support and Free Expression feels so much better. Being able to identify where you are and where you want to be is a feeling of freedom. We've touched on some ways to make that move, now let's get really practical.

Chapter Three
Making the Shift

TRUST yourself
TRUST others
TRUST the bigger picture

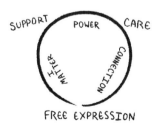

The Magic Wand

The secret ingredient to making the shift from drama to healthy relationship is trust. First you need to know there is a problem. Second you need to know that you have the solution. Third you need to take action to initiate the process and that action is **trust**. This starts as an inside job. Change your thoughts and beliefs before you rush into changing actions. We are a very action/outside oriented society, "what do I do", I'm asking you to start with "who do I be". Sometimes to remind myself I use the metaphor of standing under a tap. I can do a bunch of things to warm myself, but to be truly warm I need to go up beyond the water flow to the tap and change the temperature. Trying to change cold water at the end of its flow is frustrating, tiring and a losing battle!

The how of trust starts with unearthing the distrust. Looking at the thoughts and beliefs and thoughts behind your feelings helps us to see that they've become skewed and distorted. The mind is a powerful determiner, so if we have decided that we can't be trusted we will gather all sorts of data to corroborate this, we will unknowingly ignore evidence to the contrary. So when I am working on this myself or with other people we will lay all of the thoughts and beliefs on the table, "I cannot trust myself because this and this and this…" and then you will see the all or none thinking that is never true. We are always having a mix of experiences and we often discount the easy ones and hyper focus on the difficult. 'I can't trust anyone' will make us sort out all the trustworthy times and not give them their fair weight. Here's where choice comes in, once we can see this we can choose to be willing to trust and begin to look for the evidence to support it (trust me, it's there!!). It's also helpful to take your evidence to a higher court, whether it's a trusted wise person in your life, a spiritual teacher or a deity; when you lay evidence before them of your own or others awfulness (I do this in meditation) you will sense the untruth. Not once have I felt a "yes, it's true, you cannot and should not ever trust yourself or anyone else".

From Victim you will need to start with self-trust, believe that expressing yourself in this world matters. Believe that the answers to your problems are inside of you; that you have the right, the ability and the responsibility to guide your life. From Victim you will need to trust that EVEN IF you screw up you can try again. There is not a mistake that cannot be understood and corrected. We have heroic stories of forgiveness and recovery from even the most horrific mistakes. It requires a willingness to see that even in the situation as it exists you do in fact have power. The question to ask yourself is 'where is my power here?' What is one small thing that you can act on to get the ball rolling and drop the wall between yourself and your power?

From Bully you will need to make the leap to trust others. In connecting to others you will know how to use the power and gifts you have to be of service, to not only yourself, but to your human family and community. Your belief may be coloring every relationship and not be accurate at all, so shifting "I can't trust anyone" to "who can I trust" will usually illuminate 1 or more people who can support if they knew you needed them. This all or nothing thinking "no one likes me" "nobody cares" "everyone hates me" are characteristic of the thoughts that feed the Drama Triangle. Admitting to yourself that you need (and want) support can cause feelings of vulnerability, feeling feelings is a part of trusting. Acknowledge that even though it's hard to trust, it will be worth it. Choosing to trust will cause the ugly back stories of these positions to show up. This is cause for celebration. You are not free to choose until you know there is a choice! These ugly back stories include 'you are worthless', 'you don't belong', 'you are powerless' and they've been playing in the theatre of the mind and projected into our world for a long time. Fear will plead its case 'remember the time you trusted and it didn't work out?' to make the shift you will need to remember that you can connect to Grace, you can from a bigger point of view.

The Rescuer needs to make the leap to trusting the bigger picture. Another word for rescuer is savior and we can inadvertently believe that we are responsible for saving the world. When we think "it's all up to me" or "I have to" we are not trusting that there are other parts at play. You can realize that there is arrogance behind the rescuer! Again look at history, both personal and collective, things have a way of working out and even the biggest heroes in our stories have had support and care of others along the way. Often the Rescuer viewpoint has us looking through the microscope, hyper-focusing on the problem so that we can figure it out! Taking a step back, a breath and a new viewpoint will help us to see the larger picture, the other players and a solution that is not solely dependent on one person. Having the world on your shoulders is hard work and definitely not one you can carry on with forever. One day during my first battle with cancer, I distinctly heard an internal message "You don't have to figure it all out, it's already figured out".

Trust yourself, trust others and trust the bigger picture. Another way to put this is as a question, when you are not feeling 'good' ask yourself, what am I not trusting? This trust is a decision. This decision does not always result in an immediate outward action. Sometimes you have to make that internal decision and then let it sink in. Part of trusting the bigger picture is allowing for time to do its work. Just as the Drama Triangle reinforces the fear and separation, so does the Circle of Trust reinforce love and connection. You are building new ways of being; this has effects on the emotional, mental and physical wellbeing. Another way to think of trust is to think "if I knew the whole story I would understand". Generally our perception is limited to a small slice of information. Not knowing the back story, the lead up coupled with the inherent limitations of our sensory system mean that everything we see here is only a piece of the whole. Consider the ranges of sounds that dogs can hear that we can't and the colors that bugs can see that we don't have access to. I will believe it when I see it is limited thinking. I can consciously made the assumption that if someone is behaving in a certain way there is a reason that I am not aware of and that if I knew the whole story I would have more understanding and perhaps even compassion. My favorite example of this is The Man on the Subway – From Seven Habits of Highly Effective People by Steven Covey.

"I remember a mini-paradigm shift I experienced one Sunday morning on a subway in New York. People were sitting quietly – some reading newspapers, some lost in thought, some resting with their eyes closed. It was a calm, peaceful scene.
Then suddenly, a man and his children entered the subway car. The children were so loud and rambunctious that instantly the whole climate changed.

The man sat down next to me and closed his eyes, apparently oblivious to the situation. The children were yelling back and forth, throwing things, even grabbing people's papers. It was very disturbing. And yet, the man sitting next to me did nothing. It was difficult not to feel irritated. I could not believe that he could be so insensitive as to let his children run wild like that and do nothing about it, taking no responsibility at all. It was easy to see that everyone else on the subway felt irritated, too. So finally, with what I felt like was unusual patience and restraint, I turned to him and said,

"Sir, your children are really disturbing a lot of people. I wonder if you couldn't control them a little more?"

The man lifted his gaze as if to come to a consciousness of the situation for the first time and said softly, "Oh, you're right. I guess I should do something about it. We just came from the hospital where their mother died about an hour ago. I don't know what do think, and I guess they don't know who to handle it either."

Can you imagine what I felt at that moment? My paradigm shifted. Suddenly I saw things differently, and because I saw differently, I thought differently, I felt differently, I behaved differently. My irritation vanished. I didn't have to worry about controlling my attitude or my behavior; my heart was filled with the man's pain. Feelings of sympathy and compassion flowed freely. "Your wife just died? Oh I'm so sorry! Can you tell me about it? What can I do to help?" Everything changed in an instant."

We can start with baby steps. Trust yourself to do one little thing, or I will trust one person with this thing, or trust that tomorrow will be a better day. Looking at it like an experiment. Testing the waters and suspending judgment a moment will help you to move forward. All too often we are held immobile by fear or as I've heard it called 'faith in a negative outcome'. Just like that looking under the bed to ensure that there is no bogeyman, we need to take a big breath and take that little peak.

McDonalds Trust

I want to talk about the trust I have in McDonalds. I drive up to the drive thru, I drive ahead, I pay, I drive ahead and I get food. This is my expectation and I trust that it will happen to such a degree that when it doesn't work like that I am irritated. If the communication is not clear at 'can I take your order', if it is takes longer than I think it should or even worse if they get my order wrong I am indignant. This is the kind of trust I put in a multinational company with many moving parts and minimum wage employees! This is the kind of faith I **want** to have in myself, others and the bigger picture in addition to the compassion for when things don't work out. I want to believe that even if things don't work out immediately, eventually I will communicate my order, eventually I will get my order and if it's not right I can go back and they will make it right. I have a certainty that I will order and receive and in the big scheme of things it really won't take that long. If I could transfer the trust I have in the McDonalds Drive-Thru to the entire world I'd be in good shape!

One of the elements of the Circle of Trust is connection, use this to borrow trust! Do you have a trusting friend or someone who will walk along side of you? In my work we have called this 'the transfer of trust' and have found it very helpful in working with at risk kids who've grown to be wary of adults and new situations. We will find the person who has the greatest relationship with them, build a relationship with that person and then we can bridge a relationship with the youth. For example, a boy who has no relationships at his school but a good relationship with Mom, connect with Mom first, listen and learn and build a relationship here and the two of you work together to overcome the lack of trust in the child. Likewise we will use someone else's trust, for example if I don't trust dentists in general but I trust my friend Tammy I will ask Tammy which dentist she trusts. This is a process of reaching out. In the case of Rescuer, I can find someone who trusts the bigger picture, or a community of people and spend time with them reinforcing this idea.

The process for the Victim is a process of reaching in. This is scary and you may be afraid that you are not trustworthy. Asking for help here can also be a start point, I have used energy work for this, but know that counseling, art, music therapists and good friends can do the same. Explore expression; empty out enough to find your solutions under the mess of fears and self-attacks.

Drama is stressful, even when it's on a movie or television we can find ourselves feeling the emotional, mental and even physical effects. Continuous drama can cause what is now being caused toxic stress, all three of these Drama Triangle roles when played excessively will corrode our general wellbeing and have negative impacts on health.

Learning to break free of the drama and building connection, value and power creates a more sustainable lifestyle and more stable communities. Our body's alarm system can regulate and we become more carefree, more fun. Trust building with time and experience instead of eroding by fear.

Chapter Four
Putting it into Practice

I resist being prescriptive here and telling you what to do. I want to suggest that we are all Free Expression, you WILL find your own way to do this. With the awareness of perspective added to your unique view, you will settle on a method that makes this transition from Drama to Trust smooth. With that said, sometimes it helps to try someone else's process to get started.

So here is mine and please know that this shifts too. As Quantum physics is showing we are in constant change and motion, so a process works for a time, but as your awareness and knowledge expands your processes will shift as well. What I'm saying is rather than looking for THE WAY, as much of our literature has done, expect change, anticipate the growth, and go with the flow.

Process for Shifting from Drama to Trust
S.H.I.F.T.

Stop

It starts with a stop. It seems so simple but breaking the habit of perpetual thought and perpetual motion can be one of the most difficult steps. You need to orient to the present moment. Where am I? Take an inventory of your current landscape. Tune into all senses, including the intuitive sense, this helps bring you into the present moment and into the body. The body is an incredible communication tool, where are you stiff? Where is there soreness? The founder of Hay House Publications, Louise Hay has an incredible body of work related to the potential meanings of different body based sensations and corresponding healing affirmations.

Stopping can be incredibly difficult. The belief that things and people need our attention is persistent and well reinforced. Stopping is usually on our list, but way down at the bottom and consistently under-prioritized. Anybody who has tried meditating will know that suddenly doing the laundry or having a sandwich become incredibly important. Make a commitment to yourself to start with a full Stop. The other trick the mind will use is having you preparing to stop, putting it off until things are quiet, when you have the right pillow, after the next workshop. Just do it, just stop, here, now.

Suddenly stop is not as simple as it first sounded. Self-Awareness is a skill. Our upbringing up until now has been heavily focused on outside awareness. Pleasing others and avoiding punishment require 'other' awareness and vigilance. Self-Awareness requires inside awareness. Skills require practice, so this is something to keep at and to build, like a muscle.

Hear

Sense, what are you hearing from each of your senses? Turn your focus inward. What are you feeling? It is not uncommon for people to not even have the language for feelings, again this is an area to learn, explore and grow.

We can also be missing a sense of our own thoughts, only using those of others e.g. "he wouldn't like that". Noticing is the first step. What are you thinking? What back story is playing in there? Are there any big leaps of predicting the future? For example you find yourself thinking "if I do this, this will happen?" In truth there is no way for you to know. What is the story you are telling yourself? Take a step back and tell yourself the story, e.g. She did this and then I did that and now probably...

Highlight the blame and shame in the story, usually you will see the blame being shifted around and around until the mind find's a place where it feels most comfortable. Know that whether that blame is on you or on another there will be a loss. Guilt requires punishment and while we may think that vengeance will bring peace it does not. It reinforces the idea of a punishing mentality and therefore 'keeps us on our toes', vigilant and trying hard not to do anything wrong, hiding what we think we've done.

Orient yourself to the triangle. As you saw in the story about the Ranch you may find yourself spinning a little. Look for the dominant story. What behaviors are you seeing in yourself and others? What are you feeling, thinking and believing?

Let's talk about feeling. So much of our activity has been manufactured in order to NOT feel, avoiding negative feelings that are persistently trying to surface consumes our time. Allowing yourself to just feel takes some practice and I promise that although scary at first, it is incredibly liberating to just allow feelings to move through you. It is also faster than trying to control and hold them back. If you are angry, be angry, remembering that we are in stop so this does not mean that you act on the anger, you are feeling it.

Thought watching. Right behind the feelings are the thoughts. Capture the story without trying to judge or analyze it. Say it in your head or use your journal and write it out. Share with a trusted friend. Not for the reason of reinforcing but in the spirit of getting it out there so you can see it more clearly. 'Unpacking' is what I often call it.

Another sense to tune into is intuition. Recently I heard author Colette Baron Reid say "this is not your 6th sense; it's your first sense". Intuition is something that all of us have. We speak about it openly, this room gives me the creeps, I have a bad feeling about this, etc., and yet at the same time label it 'out there' or 'woo woo'. We see it as something that some people have and some people don't, but it is more like singing, everyone can do it, it comes easier to some and with time and attention you can build mastery in it. You are intuitive. Intuition can be put into broad categories. Clairsentience is clear feeling, another word for this is Empathic, our empathic senses help us to sense feelings. Claircognizance, or clear knowing, is that ability to 'just know' something, having something pop in your head or be certain about truth as soon as you hear it. Clairvoyance is the tendency to get intuitive information visually, not just by seeing apparitions but by catching messages in the visual surroundings- license plates, billboards, or the television. Finally, clairaudience is receiving sound information, have you ever turned on the radio and heard the perfect song to answer a question in your head? Or it can be messages that you 'hear' in your head.

Investigate

Look at the healthy aspect of the viewpoint you have sensed in yourself and know you can choose that instead. You may have to double back on sensing if you notice resistance to this. For example you see that you are in Bully and that you need connection and support, you may feel anxiety around this, and you may hear the story "NO, you can't trust anyone, don't do it". This inner story is key to changing. Sorting means that you decide what you want to keep and what you want to be done with, recognizing that these walls were built for 'protection' in a time when you thought you needed them, you know better now and there's no shame in the misperception of fear. This is where you are making the unconscious rhave found helpful in this is Byron Katie. Her book "Loving What Is" and what she calls 'The Work' are a series of 4 questions to ask regarding your thought or belief-

Is it true?

Is it really true?

How do I feel when I think this?

How would I feel if I didn't think this?

By noticing and investigating we begin to relinquish our powerlessness.   Auditing behaviors, emotions, thoughts and beliefs allow us to see where we are and from there we can choose where we are going.

Forgive

This is where the real shift occurs, you are in this viewpoint because of fear and because it served a purpose. Your past conditioning may not support a shift at all and so you need to make a leap of faith. Any new activity requires a first time and a step into the unknown. Even when we know bully or rescuer are not sustainable, helpful or productive, we may find ourselves clinging to them because they are known and because they are coping mechanisms that seemed to have worked in the past.   Forgive in this sense means to let go, to say, "oops- I was seeing this one way and now I'm willing to see it another way".   Forgive in the dictionary means to cancel, or to stop feeling anger and contempt.   In any position look at forgiving yourself and others to set up for trust, it's hard to trust if you are expecting punishment of some kind-whether you are giving it or getting it.

Trust

From Victim we need to trust ourselves.
From Bully we need to trust others.
From Rescuer we need to trust the bigger picture.

Take down that wall. To move from Bully to Support, allow support, it's there, I guarantee it, make a connection, step into the others shoes, find empathy.

To move from Rescuer to Care, allow yourself to be cared for, assert your inherent worth, you matter.

To move from Victim to Free Expression, free express, find someone and talk, journal, draw, paint, walk or dance your feelings/story.
The bottom line is getting it up and out. You will feel lighter and once it's laid out on the table you can see more clearly, gain understanding and the next step becomes obvious.

Understanding is a step towards forgiveness and forgiveness sets us free from Guilt. Guilt and Fear drive the Drama Triangle. Another way to look at understanding and when we say "I don't understand" is that there is more information needed. I don't understand is not far from "I can't stand" and requires you to either stand in your own story or get more of the other persons story. Stand there, don't let yourself flee. This is the work of it, not fixing things on the outside in the form of 'being nicer', but working at it from the inside so that your being nicer has integrity and is not a manipulation.

When we relate to one another from Care, Support and Free Expression we are sharing our power. We believe in a connection and a value in each person. This may require a different pace than we currently operate under. We may need to slow down, but I assure you that this is a "go slow to go fast" situation. When you take the time to have healthy relationships your production and actions will move ahead far quicker in the long run.

Here's how this would look. You notice that you are out of sorts. You are sad, unhappy, frustrated, depressed, etc. Rather than avoiding or comforting that feeling you are going to stop. Find a space where you can listen to your thoughts. Taking some deep breaths just do a scan and notice your senses, physicality and thoughts. Consider what you now know about the Drama Triangle and orient yourself to where you are at. For example, "Wow, I don't feel like there is anything I can do, I feel limp, tired, hopeless, this sounds like victim". From here you are just going to observe, listen to the story you are telling, watch what you are tempted to do to solve it "I'm just going to go to bed and not get up". Consider the Circle of Trust. Victim can become Free Expression. Instead of giving up right now I could express in some way. I trust myself that a solution to this problem is here, but it is hidden by a wall. You might question yourself directly, "What would happen if I did something about this?" and see what answers appear. This is a lot happening while you sit quietly, this is inner inquiry. From this place you can make a choice to change perspective. Then what? Make the choice to sit a while longer, let it settle in. "I choose to be myself, I'm going to journal until I feel better or I'm going to call a friend that will let me just vent so I can find my solution". Or you may just acknowledge that you are in victim and that's exactly where you'd like to stay for a while!! I've had that happen; it's like the country song, "I just want to be mad for a while".

The change in perspective will change us to see the situation and in turn change our behavior- now reinforcing connection and health rather than separation and fear. Once we get to see the beliefs behind the thoughts we can make a real change, we can shift.

Stop
Hear
Investigate
Forgive
Trust

Chapter Five
Cause and Effect

Eventually all roads in relationships lead back to yourself, lead back to focusing on your inner dynamics to the same degree that we focus on outer dynamics (the drama) . The basis of the framework we've been looking at is predicated on the fact that where you perceive yourself to be influences how you will see and therefore act in that situation. With this in mind it's really helpful to look at how we see our behavior and our beliefs and their effect on one another. This is another mind shift.

We have been living 'outside in', with a belief that the world has effects on us. We have reinforced this thinking for so long that it is hard to imagine otherwise. What this looks like is: this happened and now I am sad, or you make me happy, etc. I'm going to suggest that this is completely backwards, that what we believe is the cause of what we perceive. The inspiration for this 'inside out' thinking shift was introduced to me in a book by spiritual teacher David Hoffmeister, "Purpose is the Only Truth" and his work on 'Levels of Mind'.

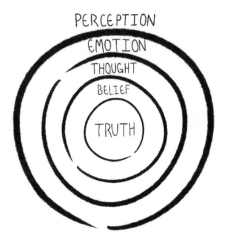

Looking at the graphic (which I've adapted from David Hoffmeister), let's consider a situation and walk through it. On the outer ring is behavior, outside world, events, stuff that happens. I'm going to use the example of my husband coming home from work in a bad mood, please feel free to insert your story as we go along.

Dusty comes home from work and he appears to be in a bad mood. Slams the door, sighs, and sets his lunch box down in a hard way. I have been working at making supper and have been in a fairly peaceful state and his mood irritates me, I think "He is wrecking the peace in here" "What is his problem?" Or maybe even "Uh, Oh, I forgot to take out that garbage" or "The kids didn't do their chores". At this point I will either correspond with a cold shoulder, a "what's your problem?" a "can I get you a drink?" or a disappearing act, depending on my mood of the day. In every way I will feel justified in the action I take and will take cues from his reaction on my next action. At some point I may even think "He is always mad when he comes home, I don't know why I married such an angry person". Now I'm going to break it down using the chart. An event happens which makes me feel a certain way, which makes me think certain thoughts which either makes or reinforces certain beliefs. This is how we are living most of the time. Reactionary, outside in, reinforcing beliefs based on external information, believing that we are ma-nipulated by outside events. This is how we most likely live our lives, and how we teach our kids to live their lives.

The paradigm shift that I am asking you to con-sider is that this is completely backwards. Even though it seems that we are affected by outside influences, the truth is that we have our cause and effect reversed. An interest-ing word play is that 'live' backwards is 'evil'. Consider it another way, instead of outside in, we consider that our beliefs cause thought patterns, which cause emotions that color how you interpret the world outside you and this in-fluences behavior. He made me mad so I …

So in this case, the behavior is slamming around, my feeling is surprise, frustration and perhaps some fear and or guilt, the story might be "I try and try and he is never happy". Here is where the real work happens be-cause we often can get to those first couple of layers and with counselling we get to the thought. The change maker is the belief. Using the process we learned in the last chap-ter, we discover that my belief is "it's a wife's responsibility to keep her husband happy". WOW, really? Can this pos-sibly be a belief that can work consistently? Do I have the power to control his mood? When I see this belief I see how insane and untenable it is, I can also see how this has been a social more and my grandparents might say 'yes, this is true'. This is where I can choose to see it differently. I can forgive the misperception that it's my job to make Dusty happy and know that I can only choose happiness for myself; this is an incredibly accelerated version of what has taken me years to get to the bottom of. So, let's look at the situation from a healthy, inside out point of view. I start with belief, this is like the metaphor of choosing which tap to turn on, I want warm water I choose the warm tap. Happiness is my choice for me. Dusty comes home and starts slamming stuff around, I can choose to ask" what's wrong?" Without the guilt and fear that it's my fault, I can hear him out. I can choose to go into the other room and take a breath if I can't seem to stay happy in the situation. I can be there for him. I can connect with myself and connect with him if I'm not lugging around the belief that his happiness is in my hands and his unhappiness is a symbol of my failure.   I don't want you to take my word for it, I ask you to expand your awareness enough to look at your recent event again and ask the question: "Was the feeling there first or was the perception of the event there first?" When we catch our perception (requires noticing and stopping mid reaction) we will often see that the feeling actually came first and if we have the ability to follow it back, like following a rope back into a cave, we will next find the thought, then the belief and finally make a conscious decision. This is about realizing our busy inner life and how it's shaping our perceptions.

I want to mention what has kept us from seeing this. First is the reinforcing nature of this system. Once I have settled on a perception I will unconsciously AND consciously gather evidence to support it. I may recall all of the other times this has happened to me, I may bring it up to friends and take in their similar stories and in this way I create a reality and justification around my thoughts feelings and actions. RARELY do we delve into belief. The practice of psychology, developing over the last 100 years has taken us deeper than before, taking us from focusing on emotion and behavior into the space of the thoughts and how the thoughts affect our behaviors. You can start with a behavior and follow it back, like following that rope back into the depth of the cave where there is less and less light, heading back to the origin of the issue, the place where you can truly affect change. You are upstream thinking, going to the headwaters. Without the will to look inside we tend to spin between emotion and perception, emotion and reaction, kept in a swirl twisted by shame and blame.

From a sense of separation, little bodies on a big planet with lots of differences, our beliefs become dual, right or wrong, good and bad, more or less. We have been reinforcing these beliefs for a long time.

From these beliefs come thoughts, THIS is right, and THIS is wrong, this is how good mothers are, this is a good relationship, this is a bad relationship and countless others. When we come to a stop we invariably notice the quantity of thoughts that are floating about in the mind. Many of my workshop participants have told me that they cannot meditate because these thoughts are too pervasive. The act of noticing and seeing these thoughts IS meditation. These thoughts are active all of the time; the decision to stop and observe them is the first step in opening your awareness to the truth and subsequently to peace. Before you can have peace it's helpful to see how NOT peaceful you are. We spend a lot of time comforting this unseen turbulence, distracting ourselves from the inner chaos with food, drama, drinks, work, relationships, etc. These beliefs lead to thoughts, which lead to emotions, separating emotions such as anxiety, anger, sadness, conditional happiness, and conditional peace of mind.

Finally, these emotions will play out in how we perceive and therefore behave in the world.

Fear has a rather limited range of behaviors, basically fight or flight. Fight can look like literal physical aggression, more often though it is verbal or passively expressed. Fight can also show up as doing, the urge to fix things. Flight can be quite literally running away or can look like freezing (like a rabbit) or appeasing (people pleasing). When we take an honest look at our behaviors it can be a little overwhelming how often we are moved to act by fear. So what are we afraid of? There are many things in the world that seem to be scary, from the tiniest of spiders to grandest of storms and that's just nature, what about each other!? Going back to the quote that 'Fear is faith in a negative outcome'. This is what this book is all about, transferring our faith from fear, the belief in a negative outcome to Love, the belief that there can be no other outcome but good. What is required is for us to see clearly and to see clearly we need all of our faculties on board and an awareness of why and how we are seeing what we are seeing.

Ultimately we are in fear of punishment, in fear that we have caused that separation or that we have been rejected and we live it out from there. `When we become aware of these beliefs we can decide whether or not we want to keep them. Whether they serve us anymore. Generally we will find them to be protective, a defense. When we act out of defense we are anticipating a battle and so that is how the world will be interpreted.

Here is a chart that you can use to capture your story; this inner work makes as much difference to your life as changing your sunglasses from blue to pink! Change the lens and you change the experience.

Telling your story from this inside out:

What happened?	How I'm Feeling?	What the thoughts are with my feelings?	What the beliefs are behind the feelings?	What I would like to believe instead?

Chapter Six
Hearts and Minds

So far we have talked about the triangle/circle frameworks for personal relationships, it can also guide leadership and management practice. In 2014 I was given the opportunity to guide a team of 'wellness coaches' to meet the need in the schools after a traumatic flood blasted the town of High River and forced weeks of evacuation. After a couple of days of team building, what I was hearing from my team was a desire to stay healthy, be present and be responsive to need. They were describing staying out of fight or flight. It occurred to me that I would be able to teach and lead from the Circle of Trust.

We used staying in the Circle of Trust; Care, Support and Free Expression to guide the 'being' part of our team. We made the decision to focus on being and allow the 'doing' to naturally emerge in response to the differing needs in the 7 schools in 2 school divisions that we served.

We recognized that we, in our chosen profession, had a tendency to fall into rescuer. With this awareness we were able to consciously remind ourselves and each other that 'we matter'. Self-care was a responsibility not a choice and frequent self and team check-ins would be expected. Watching for signs of rescuer, such as resentment and overwhelm or judgment of teachers/parents we committed to stop, breath and make another choice. Staying in Care and Support, staying warm, were the words that we used to focus ourselves when things became stressful. Allowing Free Expression in not only students but also in teachers, school staff and parents. Temptations to see youth as Victims and teachers or parents as Bullies, 'we are the only ones who understand or who get it' came up frequently. We would need to remember that if we were seeing the parents or teachers as Bullies then they needed our support not our condemnation or righteous indignation and it was a call to connect rather than judge and disengage. A guiding principal was 'you can't give what you don't have' so staying in healthy relationship with self, team and clients was considered essential.

One school in particular seemed to see us as an intrusion rather than a help. They viewed our 'openness' as 'laziness' and there were obvious signs that we were not welcome. As stated above this was a perception, and may or may not be the truth. There were explicit times for Free Expression where we recognized that we were wanting to 'set them straight (fight) or just get out and go to other schools (flight). I want to make a distinction between free expression and bitching or bellyaching. In the team atmosphere we are susceptible to feeding the Drama Triangle rather than transcending it. We had a space of trust with one another where it was understood that you could express what you were thinking as a way of getting it out so you could choose again, so that you could request care and support as needed and so that you could shift from feeling bad to feeling good. The difference being it was a constructive rather than destructive us of sharing. Using the Healthy Relationship framework we were able to de-personalize interactions and to understand what a person was looking for under their behaviors. In plain speak, if we came into a situation where a teacher or a parent were defensive towards us we were able to see that they needed connection and support rather than moving into an aggressive or collapsing place- even if it was tempting.

All employees, and myself as Program Coordinator were consistently surprised by the synchronicities that happened in those 2 years. We all felt personal growth and two staff noted to me that while we were working in a highly traumatized, disaster affected and stressful work environment their mental health was better in the job than it had been prior to coming on to the team. Our funders noted "You've done an exceptional job; you've done in 6 months what has taken other teams 6 years". By staying out of Rescuer we not only maintained our own wellness (crucial for this work) but we also did not end up in time and energy consuming power struggles with the school teams. By being healthy we were natural magnets to needy kids and we were often approached by the youth before a referral was ever sent. Our mandate was to improve mental health capacity in the schools we served and Healthy Relationships were our delivery method.

As time went by and trust grew, the school that we perceived as difficult became one of our strongest partners and we were able to do incredible work together. I look forward to seeing how this work carries forward and having the chance to influence team building and excellence in service delivery with this framework in other settings.

Chapter Seven
Healthy Inner Relationship

It's been touched on a couple of times that the Bully, Victim and Rescuer are also active inside. We may not talk about it but all of us have inner voices. Using self-awareness and mindfulness techniques we can start to hear these voices more clearly, become conscious of them rather than unknowingly allowing them to run the show.

So many of us are nice on the outside while the bully has free for all on the inside. Relentless criticism of ourselves, comparing and judging our self against impossible ideals is not abnormal. Excising this inner Bully is much of the work of counselling.

In addictions work we will often see the interplay of feeling powerless solved by some outside agent (drugs, alcohol, porn, work), then experiencing inner Bully, then inner Rescuer "it's okay, you deserve it, you've had a hard day, just have one drink" and the Victim "there's nothing I can do". Round and round.

Identifying these characters and choosing to heal them, choosing to question the back story, choosing to give them what they need (power, value and connection) can profoundly impact your outer life. You can have fun with this, give these characters names and faces. The book Taming Your Gremlin by Rick Carson has a great time with this. Come to know yourself and when these characters are most active and which outside stories SEEM to trigger them, use the inside out process to determine the beliefs that feed and enliven these viewpoints.

Inner battles between Bully and Rescuer are confusing to us and influence how we behave. Whenever we are having trouble making a decision there is some aspect of drama going on inside. Often this will bring us to an uncomfortable impasse that at its base is "I have to choose my heart or their heart", a 'damned if you do and damned if you don't', scenario. Using the triangle you can shift the inner Bully to Support, shift the inner Rescuer to Care and really be yourself, sitting in a state of Grace and acting out from there! Valuing both sides and finding their complementary aspects is the key. I see them moving from fist to fist to hand in hand. By turning inner conflict to inner harmony you will find an unconditional space of peace. This will take both the knowledge and the practice outlined in this book. I would contend that this is a great place to start, outside relationships naturally become easier when we are at ease with ourselves.

Chapter Eight
Trouble Shooting

So what happens if you know all of this and you can see it perfectly and yet you cannot seem to shift?

Usually this indicates that you are staying in the head. This is embodied work, meaning that it needs to be applied; it needs to come down into the heart, the gut, the hands and the feet. We have been a mind focused culture and can get stuck in analysis.

If you are finding yourself struggling get into your body. You can do this by noticing your senses, by grounding, or by doing something purposely physical with the intention of making a mind shift. A long walk, being outside, being with children or animals or in some kind of creative pursuit can help. There are a number of mind-body activities that can help make this process easier.

Sometimes you need to 'fake it till you make it'. Meaning that even if you don't feel like you matter, do something that acts like it, even if you don't feel connected, do something that acts like it and finally, even if you don't feel powerful, do something that someone who is powerful would do. This will take away some of the power from the inner Bully who is holding you in some kind of holding pattern with a lie. This may require a leap of faith, or a scientist mind- what do you have to lose by just giving it a shot! Again, loving the language for this, the word courage comes from the word heart- follow your heart.

Know this, you are being held by a lie. In truth you are cared for, supported and free to be you. Do not get caught up in defending your position. Defense is the first attack and a sure sign that there is drama at play. Often defense will be focused on the outside "well, honestly, I am the victim in this situation because blah, blah, blah" Once again this is about shifting on the inside, shifting how you see what you are seeing and not in shifting the outside world to fit how you want to feel.

Another block to moving forward is trying to do it all by yourself. Find a friend to share the work with, reach out to a professional if you need to, and/or connect with the Divinity that makes sense to you in prayer or meditation. Use focus tools, affirmations, crystals, posters, etc. that remind you of the Truth. You are connected. You are powerful. You Matter. You are cared for, supported and free to be you. Plant these seeds and tend to them, water them and shine the light on them, when you see the weeds of drama popping in pull them out by the root. You are the master gardener here.

Chapter Nine
Moving Forward

Are you ready? Do you have what you need to move from a life of drama to a life full of healthy relationships? Could you even come into a healthy relationship with yourself? How can you use this information? The knowledge alone allows you some choice that you may not have known you had. You can use the Circle of Trust as roots for affirmations.

I am powerful, I am connected, I am worthy, I am caring, I am cared for, I am supported, I am free to express.

You can notice when you are not feeling good and understand where you are coming from.

You can get out of constantly feeling stressed, feeling like you are in a battle, and feeling like you are moving from one problem to another.

This is meant as a way to find compassion for ourselves and others as we travel together in this world, to have the power to shift when we want to. There is no need to be limited by the past, by conditioning. This is an upgrade to your operating system.

Healthy relationships are essential to our well-being.

The idea's in this book require a mind shift, so don't beat yourself up (Bully) if you return to old patterns again and again. It is a practice and an undoing of old habits.

To sum it all up, we have been living under assumptions that are not necessarily true, most of this has been unconscious and we have been suffering for millennia. We have been competing with, defending and judging our 7 billion other human brothers and sisters and ourselves relentlessly. It's tiring and the bouts of joy are fleeting. This need not be depressing, because we also have the opportunity to challenge the paradigms that we live by we have the   ability to see and live differently.   Willingness is the key here. Willingness to trust.

We've come full circle here, back to the fact that just by picking up this book you believe that healthy relationships can exist, I look forward to seeing the fruits of our work. I appreciate your receiving my free expression.

Thank You.

Preview
The Next Shift

$\mathbf{As}$ I was saying in Chapter Four we are constantly evolving and changing. In the course of doing this work another evolution has been shared in my mind. I'm calling it the True Relationship Circle. What I'm considering is that in Truth you are a Creator supported by Unconditional Love and Freedom, you are precious, creative and a part of one grand being, and there are no walls and no limits. The Drama Triangle and the Circle of Trust remain perceptual, this shift would be to what really is.

While trust was the magic wand to get from Drama to Trust, the magic wand here is **surrender.**

Surrender your ideas about yourself, surrender your ideas about others and surrender your ideas about the bigger picture.

Surrender can be an intimidating word. What I've come to know is that we are already surrendered. We are surrendered to fear in most of our interactions. This is a choice to surrender to love, surrender to the truth of who we are. This belief that you are love may be a stretch. We are now leaning into the spiritual, into the essence of who we are.

Do not become overwhelmed by this idea, it's not one to work at. I invite you to plant the seed of this idea and be where you are at, if you are absorbing the idea of moving form Drama to Trust, awesome, this is not a race, it is a stroll and there is no reason for it to be unpleasant. At the same time some of you may be just geared this way and thinking, heck, why would I want to take the slow road? If you feel that you'd like to just live out from the Truth, then the work of it, the practice, will be choosing unconditional love and freedom in your relationships, in your being and in your doing. It's a great way to see just how controlling and manipulative our relationship practice has been!

It can seem daunting but there will come a time when you are so happy to see your patterns, so happy to see the misperception because it is here that you have power and here that control can be used most effectively. The control that was used in the outer rings to keep us falsely safe can be refocused to that inner ring. The one and only choice- separation or connection? Surrendered to fear or surrendered to love? This requires an identity check. Who are you really?

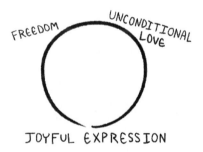

Living in Truth is the pinnacle. A place where there are only two players joined in perfect synch. These two players are you and Life. Imagine that you give and receive unconditional love, freedom and full expression with life. This would mean joy no matter what, security no matter

what and a rich tapestry of expression that is fully appreciated. This perfect dance with life, where the partnership is
based on equal power, equal voice, equal value and belonging is our Truth. It requires a dropping of all defenses, a
transparency and a full trust that we are developing. This is
the order I'm putting in, and now I will drive ahead (like I
do at McDonalds) with confidence and fully expecting to
receive.

Bibliography

1. Karpman, S. (1964). *First step for alcoholics*. Psychiatric Spectator. 1(12).
2. Hoffmeister, D. (2009). *Purpose is the Only Choice*. Living Miracles Publications.
3. Covey, S. R. (2004). *The 7 habits of highly effective people: Restoring the character ethic*. New York: Free Press

About the Author

Fawna Bews wants to figure it all out. Finding joy in pulling together the physical, mental, emotional and spiritual worlds into a casserole of satisfying and applicable practices, she also likes to just sit and look at the sky. Mother, author, leader, healer, wife and daughter are games she sometimes likes to play. Her educational life has taken her from a Bachelor's Degree in Physical Therapy to a Master's Degree in Counselling with a PhD in life as a two time cancer survivor. Find her on Facebook at Fawna Bews Connects and make sure you say hello.

Made in the USA
Charleston, SC
24 October 2016